"Los Güeros" from the Hills

"Los Güeros" from the Hills

(English translation of "Los Güeros de La Sierra")

(The term güero refers to people with light complexion and is commonly used by Latinos.)

Olivia Sosa

Library of Congress Control Number: 2023923960

ISBN: 979-8-89228-042-6   (Paperback)
ISBN: 979-8-89228-043-3   (eBook)

Printed in the United States of America

PREFACE

These stories come from interviews and recordings of my father José Sosa, who joyfully shared his many memories. Given that I organized, compiled, and edited decades of memories in his native language of Spanish, the only language he spoke throughout his life, I released this first memoir in Spanish. It has taken effort to translate and ensure that in doing so, I am staying true to the nature, charm, and context of his stories in this English version.

My father José passed away on August 19, 2013. He was 94 years old, just a couple of months short of his 95th birthday and one month short of his 64th wedding anniversary. I was fortunate to have had my father for so many years. As a young girl, I didn't know much about him other than he worked constantly trying to make ends meet, alongside my mother. Many people who I know admired and respected him because he was a generous, wise, and hardworking man. When both of our parents were working, we had our maternal grandmother, Rita, who lived with us, lovingly looking after my four brothers and me.

As an adult, I learned to appreciate the stories our father would share at family gatherings, or when something reminded him of a specific memory. In the early 2000's I began to document these stories, now I wish I had done more and asked more questions. During his last months, I recorded him so that I could concentrate more on asking him for details and clarifying questions when he was up to it.

My intent with this book is to share the sacrifices and risks my father and his brothers took, having come from very humble beginnings, to provide opportunities for a better life for their families in Mexico and the United States. These are experiences that many immigrants can relate to, but my father and his brothers had music to help them.

Amidst all the struggles and difficulties my father never complained, no matter how difficult things got. I admired this most about him, and I aspire to live my own life with gratitude and a hopeful outlook. José also had a great sense of humor, even during the most difficult times, I hope that comes through in these recollections.

In Mexico, many light-skinned people, güeros, are assumed to be from the state of Jalisco or Michoacan, and our family was no exception. In Mexico, my father and his brothers were referred to as the "güeros."

In May of 2013, my father was diagnosed with leukemia at an advanced stage. We were informed that he had approximately three months to live. We informed our family and friends and for the next three months, they came from all over to bid farewell to my father. One week before he passed, his friends from Mariachi Jilgueros came dressed in their charro outfits and brought their instruments to serenade my father. He felt so happy and excited that he asked for his violin to accompany the group. After a couple of hours, they stopped to share a meal with us. My father stated that he enjoyed himself so much that he even forgot that he was in a wheelchair! His mariachi friends returned later to accompany him at his funeral mass and the burial.

I have included a Glossary at the back of this book for the terms that I did not translate into English.

FOREWORD

By Richard Soto, founder Chicano Research Center

Reading Olivia Sosa's excellent book about her familia, Los Güeros From the Hills, was like taking a summer cruise through cool shaded mountain roads to their village near Chapala.

I feel very fortunate to have had the opportunity to be exposed to the personal life and challenges of Los Güeros. What a historic, mental trip impacted by challenges, famous personalities, and family from Lake Chapala, to Guadalajara, to Mexico City, to Cananea, to Mexicali, to Los Angeles, and finally home to Stockton, then later Elk Grove. Along the way children were born, music was written, performed, and history was recorded for us to enjoy.

I have been to Lake Chapala's water edge and its fine restaurants and purchased pottery outside of Guadalajara. I have family in Mexicali and Calexico, and as a Brown Beret, I was at the Chicano Moratorium in Los Angeles. I have lived and enjoyed the numerous entertaining musical events of Los Jilgueros.

Leopoldo Sosa, one of the Güeros, founded Mariachi Los Jilgueros in Stockton, California. Los Jilgueros entertained our community by playing at baptisms, quinceañeras, weddings, and funerals for more than four decades.

Many times, their music was donated to worthy causes, fund raisers and community events. They were there for the community which appreciated their contributions, and no wonder many of them have been inducted into the Mexican American Hall of Fame, including Jose's daughter, Olivia (the author).

Great performances occurred when Los Jilgueros were honored at the celebration at the San Joaquin Delta College in 2001, when many mariachis and the community rightfully came together to honor the original members of "Los Güeros": Leopoldo, Jose, Miguel, and Jesús Horta. Jose Sosa was honored there again in 2004. Today Los Jilgueros continues with new members and a couple of original members from the 1970's, continuing the legacy of mariachi music.

Here is where his story begins.

Life on the Ranchito

I was born on the 7th of October,1918 in the ranchito La Sabinilla, near La Manzanilla, in the state of Jalisco. I was named José when I was baptized in the church of San José de Zamora in Zamora, Michoacan, according to the document from this church, even though we lived in La Manzanilla.

Our ranchito in La Sabinilla was so small that it only consisted of two humble homes: ours and my grandfather's, Reyes Sosa. My grandfather died when I was very young, so I don't remember him well. My father's name was Remigio Sosa, and my mother was Angelita Ortega Miranda, his third wife. My mother had eight children: Refugio "Cuca" (the eldest), Ramón, María, Micaela, Miguel, myself (José), Leopoldo, and Virginia (the youngest) who died as a baby.

Shortly after Leopoldo's birth, my father was given a job at a nearby cornfield. So, we moved to a ranchito near a high knoll called Loma Alta, where my family lived until 1933. Five other families lived on these lands owned by Señor Francisco Anaya. Francisco's father owned all the surrounding land. Leopoldo was barely 40 days old; I was two, Miguel 4, Micaela 6, María 8, Ramón 10, and Cuca 11 when we left La Sabanilla.

Everyone in the family, as young as the age of six, was expected to work in the fields, planting corn, beans, garbanzo, and pumpkin. My father worked tirelessly with the crops, filling the heavy sacks, and loading them onto the boss's wooden cart, pulled by two oxen. He was paid forty centavos a day for his labor, but the children were paid ten centavos a day. Since Ramón was the eldest male, he assisted with the mares and the oxen. My father believed the landowner to be a good and generous man because he only demanded half of the harvest we collected.

All the families at Alta Loma gave him half, and everyone was expected to give him their best crop. Many times, we were left with the small, dry, black corn, so the tortillas our mother made came out black. We ate them anyway because when you are hungry you eat whatever is given to you.

Although Señor Anaya's home was large, the kitchen was small, with just enough room for the two cooks to work in. I was permitted to go into the kitchen and deliver the buckets of milk. They paid me four pesos a month for the milking, a task I enjoyed. Once in the barn, I would squeeze the teats into the bucket, but sometimes, I would sneak a few squirts into my mouth. It was such a treat – so delicious, creamy, and warm. Four months out of the year, I worked doing this until the animals were moved to another property, and I would wait anxiously for their return. Unfortunately, no one else in my family ever got an opportunity to drink the delicious milk while we lived there.

I had three half-siblings from my father's second marriage: Jesús, Nicolasa, and Andrea. Nicolasa and Andrea had left La Sabanilla by the time I was born, so I never had the chance to meet them. I did get to know my half-brother Jesús; he was tall and fair-skinned like my father, with light-colored eyes, so everyone called him "El Güero". My father's first and second wives had died during childbirth, a common occurrence in those times. Jesús had an old guitar with a missing string. He carefully hung it on a nail high on the wall so we could not reach it. However, when he was not home, my older brother Miguel would stand on a stool and play it without removing it from the wall, as we had been warned not to do. Eventually, the old guitar broke, but Ramon was able to buy us another old, used one.

Tragically, several months later in 1925, my half-brother Jesús and my baby sister Virginia died of measles. Virginia was only three months old, and we were all very distraught after losing her and Jesús.

My father Remigio told us that when he met our mother, Angelita, his family lived on one side of the river, and hers on the other side. This could have been what they called the Passion River, which forms a part of the border between Jalisco and Michoacán. In the evenings, Angelita's father would call out to my father, "Remigio, come over and sing to us." He would sing whenever he had time, and eventually, my parents got to know each other and later married. I wish I had had the opportunity to hear my father sing or play the guitar, but as a husband and father, he used all his time and energy to work and support his family.

When I was almost 8 years old, I was in a serious accident. I was playing with my brothers and some friends with a homemade cart built by my brother Miguel out of discarded boards and metal wheels. There were six of us playing and everyone had taken their turn riding the cart down the hill. When it was finally my turn, Miguel instructed me to sit on my knees and to hold on to the boards on each side. He yelled, asking if I was ready, and then he pushed me down the hill. The cart started gathering speed quickly, and suddenly it rolled over a large stone. I felt a sharp pain and realized that my little finger had gotten smashed between the metal wheel and the stone. I screamed and the girls who were standing nearby, Angelina, Mónica, and Petra, came running to see what had happened. They saw my bloody finger and told me that it had been chopped off, so I cried even louder. Señor Jose Gutierrez, a close family friend, heard the commotion and ran over to us. He noticed that the tip of my finger was still attached, so he grabbed a strip from an agave plant and wrapped my finger tightly. He carried me home and patiently explained to my father what had happened, making an unsuccessful attempt to protect Miguel, who was supposed to have been taking care of me. My father removed the strip and saw the small bone sticking out of the skin, so he forced it back in place and retied it.

Eventually, my pinkie healed, but I never removed the strip of agave so it must have dissolved. My finger has looked strange all my life from that incident, with an extra stub at the end. Fortunately, it never affected my left hand and how I played the violin.

Another injury I survived occurred when I was 10 years old while I was chopping firewood with my father's ax. While trying to chop a very thick stump, I raised the ax high to strike it with all my force. When I hit the stump, the blade bounced off and landed on my left calf, cutting a long gash. Blood was gushing all over my leg. I was alone and afraid, so I hid where no one could see me cry. After a while, I calmed down and walked home slowly, trying to hold on to my calf to stop the bleeding. When I arrived home, my father examined my leg and tied it up, but he never scolded me as I had feared. I have had that scar on my leg all my life, and sometimes when I see it or touch it, I recall the incident.

The Harp

My father was also a carpenter, and he was inspired to make a harp for Leopoldo with his rudimentary tools. He had purchased some strings for it from the Tarascan Indians. The Tarascans would walk for five days to come down from the mountain to sell their crafts. However, when he completed the harp, the 35 strings did not fit exactly as they should have, but Leopoldo played it as best he could.

One day while I was working in a garbanzo field, a man approached me and asked, "Do you know how to sing?" He said he would pay me one centavo for each song I sang. I answered, "Yes, I sing, and so do my brothers." So, I went to find them. Miguel, Leopoldo, and I sang four songs, and he paid us four centavos. This was the very first time we were paid to perform music.

I treated myself to two tasty sweetbreads from a neighbor with my part of the earnings.

One time a neighbor came around to cut our hair, and he brought along an old violin. He let me borrow it, so now all three of us had instruments: Leopoldo the harp, Miguel the guitar, and I the violin. We had to make the strings for our instruments from animal guts. At night we hunted for skunks, which was difficult, and when we returned home early in the morning, the smell was horrible. We removed the guts and hung them out to dry in the sun. We kept an eye on them as they dried so that we could stretch them regularly until they were the thickness that we needed. We also used the guts of old dogs when they died. This was the way things were done in those days.

As my father Remigio got older, he enjoyed sitting out in the evenings to rest and to listen to us sing and play our instruments. Leopoldo was so small that when he sat on the bench to play the harp, his feet would dangle. The breezes would carry our music to the neighbors, who all enjoyed it so much that they decided to gather their money and ordered a real harp for Leopoldo. The man who made harps lived on the other side of the mountain, and he wanted fourteen pesos for the parts and labor. A few weeks later, we were sent to pick up the harp. My sister Micaela's husband, my cousin Salvador, Pancho, and I left early in the morning. We did not arrive at the man's house until nighttime and when we did, we surprised him because he had not finished the harp. He suggested we rest and sleep on the floor because he needed to work all night to complete it. I was exhausted and tried to sleep, but I was also hungry — we had not eaten since breakfast. When I finally fell asleep, I dreamt of food, and I think my cousin did, too, because I heard him making chewing sounds in his sleep. We woke up early in the morning and began our trek back home. Once again, we walked all day, but now we were carrying a bulky and heavy harp, so we took turns carrying it. When we got home that evening, we were starving after not having eaten for almost two days.

Daily Life

Life was very hard in those days and food meant survival. There were times when our family would run out of food and the owner would lend us the sacks of corn we needed. For the first 100 kilos he demanded repayment of double what he had lent us. If we needed more than 100 kilos, he would charge us triple the amount. Unfortunately, this happened several times.

The water we used for our household, came from two natural springs. Occasionally, they would dry up, and Leopoldo and I would have to travel further to obtain the water. To ensure that we always had access to water, my father decided to move the family and build a house closer to another water source. He built a one-room adobe house, and later he added another room as the kitchen. All of us kids slept in the kitchen, on the floor, on top of petates. He added a large built-in comál to the corner of the kitchen, made from a flat metal piece. My mother fed firewood underneath the comál to heat it for cooking. Our basic diet consisted of beans and corn tortillas, as well as the few vegetables we grew. After a couple of years, all the families from the ranchito came together to build a small dam for easier access to the water we all needed.

A capulín fruit tree grew near our house and it produced dark, sweet, red berries, like a black cherry tree. When the berries turned black, they were ripe and ready to eat. My brothers and I picked and enjoyed the ripened, grape-size sweet berries. It was a rare treat for us to have something sweet to eat.

Death was very common in our rural area. My family didn't have access to medical care, like that which was offered the cities, nor the technology that people can utilize today. When folks got sick, they were usually treated with home remedies.

I recall one of my best friends dying suddenly. We had been playing and running around outside when a scorpion near a rock stung his leg. His father came running when we told him what had happened, but he was unable to do anything to save him. The next day the boy died, and my father agreed to build him a small coffin. The following day I was planning to accompany my father to deliver the coffin, but I had hurt my hand with his tools, so he made me stay home as punishment for being careless. This was going to be my first real funeral because I couldn't recall the one for my brother Jesús nor my baby sister Virginia.

A few months after my friend died, I was working alongside my brother Ramón in the field about a mile from our home. As I reached down to pull a weed, a scorpion bit me on the middle finger of my right hand. My first thought was, "I'm going to die!" I ran to Ramón who was with the oxen, and he told me that he couldn't leave. He ordered, "Go home quickly!" I started walking down the hill, but I began to feel dizzy and nauseous. When I could no longer walk, I sat next to a large gate where people frequently passed by. I was there for what seemed like an eternity, thinking I was going to die right then and there. It just so happened that nobody walked by that day! About two hours later, Ramon arrived at the gate. "What are you doing here?" he yelled. I could not speak so I began to cry. Ramón lifted me and carried me all the way home. My mother made viper tea. According to her, it was a remedy for scorpion bites, and she forced it down my throat. I consumed this for three days because I couldn't eat anything. My throat felt like I had a spider web stuck inside, but little by little I began to feel better. I do not know how I survived. People believed that it depended on where the scorpion bit you, if you survived or not. I was so grateful that God had saved me again.

A Mariachi is Formed

My brothers and I learned to play music by ear, listening to and watching other musicians, because we did not know how to read music. The first songs we learned were "Angelitos del Cielo" (Angels of Heaven), "La Fuerte de Lolita" (Strong Lolita), and "Las Barandeles del Puente," (The Bridge Rails). One day a neighbor informed us about the annual festival in the town of Sayula. He said we could earn some pesos playing there, so we decided to try our luck. We walked for a full day to Saluya, carrying our instruments. Leopoldo was still very young, so Miguel carried his harp, and I carried the violin and guitar. Our excitement as we headed to the festival made the journey bearable. Shortly after arriving, we were approached by a lady who offered us a shot of pulque. I said "yes" not knowing what to expect. I took a swig and enjoyed the warmth as it slid down my throat. We performed at the festival for two days, taking advantage of any opportunity to play. We earned fifteen pesos that weekend, playing night and day, and on the way home, we stopped to visit our maternal grandmother. She made sure we ate plenty because we still had a long distance before we reached our house.

When I was 13 years old, we met a man named Felipe who said he knew how to play the harp and the guitar, so my father asked him to come and teach us what he knew. He came for just a couple of weeks, and each time he brought along his brother Rubén. Felipe did not teach us much that we didn't already know, so we told our father to fire him, and he agreed. We were glad to get rid of him because our poor mother had to feed both, and we barely had enough food for our family. Also, Felipe liked to stare at our sisters, and we were very protective of them. My father paid him with corn; but instead, he asked us to work for him for a week. It turned out that he was quite lazy too, so when we finished working his portion of the fields, we never saw him again.

Later that year, an elderly man visited us from another ranch to tell us that his son was getting married and that he needed musicians for the celebration. The musicians he wanted to hire had a previous engagement in another town, and they could not guarantee to return in time for the ceremony. It was tradition that the night before a wedding celebration, all the women gathered to grind corn, cook the chicken mole, and make tortillas. Early the next morning, two women came to lead us to their ranch. My father warned the women that we did not know too many songs, but they said it did not matter since there were no other musicians and the couple was expected soon. They agreed to pay us three pesos and Leopoldo and Miguel left with them. I, on the other hand, refused to go and no one could convince me, so our cousin Salvador went in my place.

Later that morning, Leopoldo came back for me. He complained, "José, we can't play with Salvador, and we need you to help us." I felt I did not have a choice and agreed to go with him. When we arrived, we saw the newly married couple coming down the road on their horses. There was yelling and gunshots being fired as they approached. We started playing at once, prepared to greet the couple. The cooks had placed long wide boards on the ground for the guests to eat. Everyone squatted to eat the beans, rice, and mole that was served on the boards. The mole is called *Mancha mantel* (tablecloth stainer) because it is red and sweet, and commonly stained tablecloths and clothes. The other musicians arrived soon after and I thought, "How are we going to compete with these professionals?" So, we stopped playing and they took over providing the music. I snuck up the hill to hide, but as soon as I did my stomach began to growl so I returned to eat with everyone else. During one of their breaks, one musician asked to look at Leopoldo's harp. He strummed it and then complemented Leopoldo saying,

"Your harp is very well-tuned." I imagine he was surprised and assumed that we did not know very much about music. The father of the bride generously paid us three pesos even though we only played for part of the day. My favorite memory about that day was the delicious meal, we rarely ate mole!

After the wedding, another neighbor, Felipe Pichardo, came to ask us to serenade his wife because he wanted to surprise her for her birthday. However, the gossip amongst the neighbors was that his wife was bewitched because she never left her house. We ignored the rumors, as this was another opportunity to earn pesos. We serenaded her outside the window all night, but she never came out. Finally, the husband apologized and said, "My wife believes that she has a piece of corn stuck in her throat and doesn't want anyone to see her, so that is why she refuses to come to the window. I had hoped that she would consider looking out to listen to the music." Felipe was a merchant who sold eggs and Fabric. He charged a centavo and a half for each egg. As payment, he gave us two dozen eggs and several yards of fabric. My sisters were pleasantly surprised, and Cuca exclaimed, "We have enough fabric for two skirts!" Our mother was most pleased with the eggs, a rarity in our diets.

During this time, I was earning fifty centavos a day for working in the fields, which was hard labor. The worst were the stiff dry husks that would cut up my hands. As I was leaving the field one day, a man yelled at me, "I hear that you and your brothers are musicians. Do you want to buy a violin?" "How much do you want? " I replied as I moved closer. I agreed to purchase it for seven pesos which meant fourteen more days of work to save up for it. However, we finished the field in only 13 days, which meant that I was fifty centavos short. Thankfully, the man was kind enough to sell me the violin anyway and when I was able to make more money, I paid the rest of what I owed. Despite all my hard work, someone accidentally stepped on the violin and snapped it in half. The next one that I purchased cost me twenty pesos, which meant more days of work.

Changes in the Family

My sisters Cuca, Micaela, and María all got married and left the house within a year. Cuca married a good friend of the family, José Gutiérrez. After their ceremony, Gutiérrez came on his horse with a bottle of tequila, firing his gun up in the air. I was frightened until I realized who it was. Gutiérrez jumped off his horse and offered me a drink, but I said no. He then offered the tequila to Miguel who, without hesitation, said yes! Gutiérrez was a handsome, tall man, with blue eyes like Cuca's, and two of their daughters were also born with blue eyes. Gutierrez was a good man and a good husband and lived almost to a hundred because he was very strong and healthy. One of their sons, Manuel, married a girl named Josefina. They knew each other but hadn't had an opportunity to speak much. However, one Sunday afternoon Manuel passed by Josefina's house. Since she was outside, he took the opportunity to talk to her. After talking for a while, they heard a racket and looked up to see three men on horses approaching her house. Josefina yelled, "Those men are coming for me! " She ran into her house and returned with a pistol which she handed to Manuel. He held the gun up and when the men saw it, they turned their horses around and left. Josefina cried to Manuel "They are going to come back for me, so you have to take me with you!" They ran away, got married, and eventually had six children, several with blue eyes. My eldest brother Ramón also married at that time and moved away. After that, there were only three of us living at home, and since Miguel was now the eldest male, he was now responsible for the oxen.

Education

There were no schools near us so the families of our ranchito gathered 25 signatures to request a government teacher. When the teacher arrived, she realized that we didn't have a schoolhouse, but the parents had built a set of crude benches and placed them under the trees. The teacher had brought a large chalkboard, so that completed the school. Leopoldo was 12 years old, and I was 14 when we attended school for the first time. Because my father needed us to help him out in the field regularly, we had to miss many school days. Despite our absence, we did manage to learn the names of the letters, the sounds, and the numbers. First, I memorized the vowels in order: A, E, I, O, U, but one day the teacher changed the order of the vowels, and when I read aloud, "A, E, I, O, U, she scolded me. After that, I committed to seriously study the letters and their sounds to be able to read. I already knew how to count to one hundred, working in the fields and counting centavos, but I did not recognize the numbers. The teacher wrote the number 4 on the board and then asked me, "What number is this?" When I didn't know, she said I had to study with Leopoldo, who was learning quickly.

Somehow, we passed the first year and learned to read a little and write the numbers and our names. The following year we returned, but we had missed too much of the school year already. We realized how far behind we were when the teacher handed us a book full of rows of words and neither of us could read it. We decided not to return because we could not attend consistently. Miguel never went to school because he was older, and he helped in the fields every day. Leopoldo was very intelligent and taught Miguel what he had learned. Given our lack of education, we could not have imagined that in the future we would all have children who would become teachers, administrators, scientists, and professionals.

Political Conflicts

In México, there was a conflict known as **La Cristiada,** lasting from 1926-1929, between the government and the faithful followers of the Catholic church, The government aimed to eliminate the power of the Catholic church and President Plutarco Elías Calles changed the Mexican Constitution of 1917 to enforce the new laws against the church. The **Cristeros** were the religious personnel and the public who fought against these laws and wanted to restore the power of the church. The president's federal army was ordered to close the churches and prohibit religious services. Without the Catholic church, the people could not baptize their children and church weddings could not be held. One day the Cristeros arrived at our ranchito and told us that they would hurt us if we disobeyed them. They took our livestock and harvest, and even searched our homes to take whatever food and supplies we had. My mother had wrapped our tortillas in a cloth and buried them beforehand, or else they would have taken those too. It was a terrible time, and we were all very afraid. When they finally departed, we were left with nothing and we had to start all over again to survive, in very lean times. Mr. Anaya helped by bringing more animals, corn, and seeds.

Another conflict involved new federal laws declared by the President of México, Lázaro Cárdenas, for agrarian reform. The federal **Agraristas** were assigned to enforce these new laws. President Cardenas expanded the agrarian reform and ordered that the country's peasants be granted the land on which they worked. It is estimated that between the years 1934 and 1940, more than 20 million hectares were redistributed to the peasants, over 49 million acres. (**1. Wikipedia**). The families in our ranchito who wanted a parcel of land were required to travel to Guadalajara to submit their request for ownership in person. A group of agraristas arrived at our little ranch to enforce the new agrarian reforms and approached my father.

They demanded that he sign a document requesting his parcel of land, but my father refused to sign. Then they informed him that we had eight days to leave the property. My father felt that if he signed, he was betraying the boss, who had always been kind to us. The year was 1933, and my father decided to take us to the town of Chapala.

Leaving Our Ranchito

We left our ranchito on a Saturday morning, and walked to the shore of Lake Chapala, by the little town of Tizapán del Alto. We carried our loads consisting of a few clothes, a sack of corn, some tools, and our instruments. It was just Leopoldo, Miguel, me, and our parents. We were the three teenagers left at home, the other siblings had married and left the ranchito years prior. Some years later they would also come to live in the town of Chapala. When we arrived at the shore, we boarded a large sailboat because it was the only one available that night. It was a cargo boat full of lumber and animals, and we had to crowd onboard. We sailed all night, and it was a very uncomfortable trip and our poor mother suffered greatly. The sail was carried by a wind called *The Mexican* because it originates from Mexico City. Every time the boat swayed, I feared falling off and drowning. The light of the moon shone over the water, but I saw nothing all around us in the darkness. Lake Chapala is the largest lake in Mexico, it is located at almost 1500 meters altitude (almost 5000 feet) and is surrounded by hills and volcanic rock mountains. **(2. Wikipedia)** The town of Chapala is 45 kilometers (about 30 miles) from the city of Guadalajara, making it a popular destination for tourists during the weekends and holidays. My family had never traveled so far, and the unknown was frightening. We had no idea what life would be like for us in Chapala.

Cargo sailboat

Miguel, José, and Leopoldo as teenagers.

Music in Chapala

We arrived in Chapala on a Sunday morning and dozens of people were waiting to purchase the boat's cargo. We asked around for Mr. Anaya, who was related to our boss in Loma Alta. Mr. Anaya owned property near Chapala and he had promised to give us work. He was a generous man and provided us with work and with a room to house us, near the center of the town of Chapala. We joined his other workers in the tomato, chili peppers, onion, corn, and bean fields. Miguel, Leopoldo, and I continued to help our father every day. Leopoldo was such a good worker that he impressed a man, Aurelio, who one day approached my father. "I like the way your son Leopoldo works, and I would like to buy him from you." My father, in shock, responded, "Of course not!" We did well the first year, but the following year resulted in a very poor harvest. When my father traveled to Guadalajara to sell it, he was offered very little for it. As a result, we had very little food and often went hungry, especially now that the three of us were all growing young men.

We lived in crowded conditions in our little room, but we were grateful to have a place to call home. My poor mother had to grind the corn and cook outdoors in the sun to make our food and tortillas. The guava tree in the backyard was too small to provide her with any shade. We continued playing our music and when we practiced indoors in the evenings, sometimes passersby could hear us. Unfortunately, when the police heard us, they would bang on the door and order us to stop or else we had to provide a permit to play. We always stopped and responded by saying, "We were just rehearsing." They informed us that we needed a permit even to do that! After a while, ensuring that they had left, we would continue.

Photo of old Chapala

Andrea

A neighbor of ours was a middle-aged woman named Andrea. She was a singer, and her husband was a sailor who accompanied her on his guitar. Andrea dressed in trousers and wore a hat, so people did not realize she was a woman. One day, before one of her scheduled performances, Andrea had quarreled with her husband. She left him and came looking for us. Andrea invited us to eat pozole and asked us to bring our instruments. We were not sure about the invitation, but we were not about to refuse a delicious meal. I hesitated for a minute because I realized we had to haul along the heavy harp. After our meal, we followed her around the lake. She knew where the parties were and where we could earn pesos. She charged one peso per song, and at the end of the day, she distributed the earnings among us. We realized, for the first time, that we could supplement our field earnings with music in this tourist-rich town.

One day Andrea took us to a fancy restaurant-bar at the lake's edge and she introduced us to the owner, a very sophisticated lady. One of the waiters heard us practicing during Andrea's break and asked us if we knew one of his favorite songs. We did, and we played it for him, along with two other songs. He gave us four pesos, not realizing that we were only going to charge him 50 centavos for each song. The waiter encouraged us to learn more songs to entertain the tourists from Guadalajara, who flocked to the lake and its restaurants on the weekends. We learned to first approach a group of tourists, play a set of songs, and then inform them how much they owed us. Surprisingly, it worked!

Music in Chapala

There were three mariachi groups in Chapala, including ours, of which Andrea was a member. One group was called Mariachi Grande. I wanted to join their group, but they rejected me. One of their members told me that I could follow them around and play with them, but that I was not going to get paid until I learned their arrangements. I decided against it. The groups in town had heard us practice and began to invite us to play with them when they needed a musician. Leopoldo was now playing the guitarrón so if they needed a guitar or guitarrón, Miguel or Leopoldo would go, but when they were missing a violin, it was my turn. We became friends with the other musicians, and they began to call my brothers and I, the *"güeros"* from the hills, (*the fair ones*) because we had told them we came from Loma Alta. Soon other musicians came along to join our group. However, they did not want Andrea, so we had to let her go. In those days females were not in mariachis. We were grateful for all that Andrea had taught us and were sad to see her go.

Left to right: Esteban Hernández, his father José Hernández, José Sosa, child – the group's first trumpet player, my brothers Leopoldo Sosa and Miguel Sosa, and another partner.

Esteban Hernández was one of our first recruits. He and his father were both violinists with another mariachi, but one day Esteban informed his father that he wanted to join the *güeros*. "Well, if you go, I'll go too." his father responded. Leopoldo agreed, and they began to play with us and now our group consisted of seven members, with a second guitar player and a youngster who played the trumpet. We were now the new Mariachi Grande!

Our Own Home

Miguel, Leopoldo, and I combined our earnings intending to build a house for our family. One Sunday alone we earned 14 pesos, which we added to our savings and made enough for the down payment on a plot of land we had selected. The plot cost 500 pesos, so we bought it and agreed to pay 20 pesos monthly. Every month Miguel made the payment in person. It took us six years to pay it off, and we were finally landowners, something that would not have happened had we remained in our old ranchito.

Every Sunday morning the cargo sailboat, like the one we had used to cross the lake, arrived loaded with lumber, pigs, goats, and tools. We had worked extra hours that weekend, so Miguel purchased lumber for the roof. We finished the roof, built the windows, and added a large porch to complete the house.

We were still residing in the little room that Mr. Anaya had provided for us, but now we paid rent because we could afford it. My father was no longer able to walk, so he couldn't work. On the day we finished the house, we carried him to see it, followed by our mother. When our father saw it, he began to cry and said, "Forgive me, I wish I had been able to help you."

Our mother was very happy with her indoor kitchen. Together as a family, we enjoyed our new little house for a year before our father died. I recently found out that he died at the age of 74, I thought he was over 80. Fifteen days after his death, our mother died, she was only 54. We were shocked because earlier in the day she had complained about a painful stomachache. She drank an herbal tea, but within hours she passed away. We remained in our house, but now we were alone, with no parents. My brothers and I were still working for Mr. Anaya during the week, but when he found out that our mother had died, he asked, "What are you going to do now? You do not have anyone to cook for you, no one to make you tortillas." He said we couldn't work without food during the day, so he fired us.

He was right, now we had to buy tortillas and sometimes our neighbors brought us tacos. None of us knew how to cook.

Now that we no longer worked for Mr. Anaya, we focused on obtaining more musical gigs. The largest cantina in town was called the Beer Garden, located outdoors on the shore of Lake Chapala. There the waiters served lots of alcohol to the tourists who came to relax and enjoy the lake and the music. During the years 1935-37, we were a very busy mariachi.

Our mariachi decided to travel to Guadalajara to seek more work, but after arriving we quickly realized that the city was already full of mariachis. However, we found an outstanding trumpet player, Jesús Horta, and invited him to join our group. Jesus returned to Chapala with us, and we decided to officially change our name from Mariachi Grande to Mariachi Chapala. Leopoldo was now only playing the guitarrón, the big bass guitar since it was a lot easier to haul around.

Playing for tourists at the Beer Garden by Lake Chapala.

Mariachi Grande with violins: Esteban Hernández, José Sosa, another violinist, José Hernández (father of Esteban), Miguel Sosa, and Leopoldo Sosa.

The Border

At the age of 19, I headed north to attempt to cross the border into the United States. Everyone at home warned me not to go, saying, "You're crazy, it's too dangerous!" Nonetheless, I boarded the train in Guadalajara and arrived at the border two days later, near El Paso. I walked around wondering how to go about crossing into the States. I approached, what I perceived as a friendly-looking man who said, "Go to the river at night, and there you will see the people who can help you." It was not dark yet, but I walked to the river anyway. No one was around so I waited until dark. I could not believe how many men, with boats of all kinds, were waiting and ready to help those of us who wanted to cross, for a price, of course!

I saw two men who were standing by a small rubber raft, and I asked them how much they charged. I paid them 20 pesos to take me across and once on the raft, they handed me an oar. One of the men demanded, "You have to help us paddle," so we all did. It was a moonless night, and I began to feel anxious while observing the river's strong current. Suddenly, we realized that there was a leak in the raft! I was not confident in my swimming skills, so I panicked even though it appeared that we were close to land. It is one thing to swim in the waters of Lake Chapala and it is another thing to swim in a fast-moving river. The man behind me grabbed a bucket and threw it at me. We began to bail out the water while the front man paddled furiously. I thought for sure I was going to die here, but God saved me yet again.

Finally, we reached the opposite bank of the river. Trucks were lined up, waiting for those of us who had successfully crossed. I was exhausted and trying to catch my breath when I heard a man ask me if I wanted to work. I agreed and followed him to his truck, along with three other men who had climbed in. It did not occur to any of us to ask for details. We didn't ask where we were going, nor how much we were going to get paid, or not even what we were going to do. The man drove for over an hour before we reached a ranch. There were about 30 of us there, and at night we slept in a large barn. They provided us with three meals a day, for which we were charged. Sundays were our day off, and some of the men purchased beer and cigarettes at the ranch store to enjoy the day. I worked there for a month and a half, but I decided that I didn't want to stay there any longer. I spoke to the supervisor, who had picked us up at the river, and informed him that I was leaving. He told me to wait until Sunday morning so that he could drop me off by the highway. It was still dark that morning when we left. He paid me, dropped me off and wished me luck. I thanked him and began to walk down the highway.

I walked for a while when a semi-truck stopped and asked me if I wanted a ride. I replied yes and informed him that I was headed to México. He laughed, exclaiming, "Then you are on the wrong side of the road!" "Oh, no!" I exclaimed, "Thank you." I crossed the highway and continued my journey. Since it was so early, there weren't many cars on the road, but soon another truck came by. I hopped in, and he drove me down to the border. When I arrived, I walked up to the immigration office and saw that it was closed, so I sat and waited for it to open. When the Border Patrol officer arrived, he asked, "What are you doing here?" I told him I needed to get to Mexico. "That's funny!" he exclaimed. "Everyone wants to come to the States, and you want to leave!"

Once in Mexico, I bought a train ticket to Guadalajara. When I arrived in Chapala, everyone was surprised to see me. They thought that they weren't ever going to see me again. Despite my misadventure, the idea of returning to the United States never left me.

Mexico City

Back at home, I began playing with the Mariachi Chapala again. In 1941, we took our mariachi to Mexico City for the first time. We would stay for two or three months, save our earnings, and then return to Chapala. I decided to remain in Mexico City and for the first time I was alone in the city, I headed to the famous Garibaldi Plaza to look for work in a popular cantina called El Tenampa.

Members of the musicians' union kept an eye out for any new musicians arriving at Garibaldi Plaza. They took turns supervising the square, and when they spotted a new arrival, they would inquire about their membership status. Musicians who were not union members were asked to leave.

Union membership meetings were held every Thursday, and the new guys were invited to join. Despite the union control, mariachi groups didn't seem to care whether musicians were union members or not when they needed a musician. One time a group invited me, and I told them that I was not a union member. They simply said, "It's fine, just go to the corner and we will pick you up there." And off we went. This happened regularly.

A trick we used to obtain work was to approach a car and start playing. We would yell, "Look how nice we play!" Sometimes we were hired like that and ended up playing at a park or at their parties. I would earn three or four pesos an hour, and that is how I survived in the big city. Many groups allowed me to work with them and things went well, so I decided to become a union member. I became a member and continued to be one, even later when I worked in the United States.

When I returned to Chapala, Mariachi Chapala did not need another violinist so once again, I had to work with other groups. But when Mariachi Chapala decided to go on tour, they invited me to rejoin them. We would be on tour for about three months and then return home to Chapala for a week's break, or until we needed to earn more money. Between the years 1941 and 1943, we had many challenges and difficulties while on tour, yet we remained together and persevered.

In 1943, Leopoldo married a young girl named María in Chapala. She moved into our house, so María and Leopoldo had one of the bedrooms, and Miguel and I had the other. María would clean, cook, and do the laundry for the three of us. Her mother would arrive early to help her with these chores. The situation seemed unfair to me, so I moved out, concluding that María had only married Leopoldo, not all three of us. I headed back to Mexico City, but this time my goal was to sign up as a bracero in the United States.

From Musician to Bracero

World War II had begun, and most American men were now serving in the military. In 1942, the United States announced a project called the Bracero Program, to recruit farm laborers. Mexico City was one of the designated sites for recruitment, so I traveled there with seven other men from Chapala. I was told that we were among the approximately 300,000 men who had arrived at Mexico City. However, we knew that the United States had only sent 50,000 tokens to the city. The applicants who had arrived first were given tokens by the Americans but by the time we arrived, all the tokens had been distributed. The men with tokens would gather around the national stadium entrance. These men waited for the daily announcements to hear which color of token was going to be admitted. They would line up to get inside the stadium and begin the examination process.

My friends and I were sitting at a nearby park wondering what to do next since we hadn't arrived in time to get a token. We were approached by a gentleman who asked us if we had already purchased our tokens. I said that we didn't know that purchasing them was an option. He informed us that he had a connection with someone who printed counterfeit tokens. We were interested. Why not? It was worth a shot! We followed him to a hotel where we met his partner. He said, "I can make you eight tokens for a thousand pesos." We agreed to the price and combined our funds to pay him. Even though we were nervous about the deal, we felt we had no other choice. We had traveled all this way, and this seemed like the only alternative left. We heard that the tokens were going for 100 pesos each, but we were already committed to the man in the hotel. When we returned after two days, to pick up out tokens, the gentleman wasn't there! I felt my heart drop and thought we had been swindled. Fortunately, we found a message from him indicating that we should return the following day. We were so relieved when we had those tokens in our hands. Before we left, he recommended that we rub the tokens so they would look worn.

Men waiting to be braceros.

A hundred pesos was a lot of money in those days and the police, who patrolled the stadium, would use any excuse to harass the men and steal their tokens. Then the corrupt police officers would turn around and sell the tokens for 100 pesos to someone else. I recall that one of our companions, Polonio, began complaining about having to wait so long. I didn't blame him. We had been

Jose age 25

sleeping in the park for a week, spending money on food and water, and just sitting around. Polonio finally decided that he'd had enough, and sought someone to buy his token, so he could return home. The word got around and soon a potential client approached him and asked about the token. Polonio said he would give him a deal and sell it to him for only 75 pesos. "Can I first see your token?" the stranger asked. When Polonio handed it to him, the man grabbed it and ran! Polonio, shocked, ran after him, and we followed. We were unable to catch the thief, and poor Polonio had to return home empty-handed.

The tokens came in three colors: blue, gray, and white, and one color was announced each day. Finally, my color, gray, was announced and I ran straight to the stadium to get in line. Each day the stadium doors were opened promptly at eight in the morning but closed only an hour later. Only those who could be processed at that hour were allowed in. I had been informed that the men who did not have tokens just stood in line to save the place for someone else and that they charged a couple of pesos for this service. I approached a man and asked, "Hey, will you let me have your place in line?" "Yes, but it will cost you," he said. I gave him five pesos and took his place in line near the front, even though I was there one day ahead of my time to report. Other men had the same idea, and the line began to grow, and all were beginning to crowd and squeeze from behind. I stood by the wall all night without being able to move, afraid of losing my place. By morning, when the doors were opened, there appeared to be another line of men, right next to the wall! Turns out that during the night the men who had not been in line during the day had climbed the wall and as they dropped themselves down, they pushed out to those of us who were already lined up. I was no longer next to the wall, and I felt angry and frustrated. I saw a police officer approaching and striking the men who were not by the wall with his baton and pulling them out of the line. It was not worth getting hit and even risk losing my token, so I got out of the line and looked for a place to sit and think. I was feeling depressed and decided to go for a walk around the stadium to help me think and figure out what to do next.

When I reached the other side of the stadium, I saw a group of men beating on the stadium brick wall with rocks. I was astonished that they thought they could make a hole in the wall and thought, "These guys are crazy!" I walked around the stadium again, and when I got to where the men had been, I saw that they had made a hole in the wall!

I cautiously glanced through it and spotted a police officer inside who was conducting training exercises. There was a large group of men on the first floor and another group of potential braceros on the second-floor balcony, most of them wearing sombreros. Since the policeman's back was to me, I decided to take a chance and go for it. I paused and thought, "If he catches me, he'll steal my token, but oh well!" I climbed over the bricks carefully, so as not to make noise. I was almost inside when a large brick tumbled over. Of course, the officer heard the noise. He turned around and began yelling, "Stop! Stop I say!" as I ran as fast as I could. I tried to hide in the crowd. I decided to climb a metal pole to the second floor and hide there. Once on the second floor, I crawled around a sea of legs. One man looked down and laughed exclaiming, "Damn, he almost got you!" I moved to the group of men on chairs and sat on an empty one, assuming that I was no longer being followed. The man next to me said, "Look, I got in yesterday, the men who came in today are down in that group. He volunteered to help me and said, "The bathrooms are down there by where those two police officers are standing. They will ask us where we are going, and I will say we are going to the bathroom. You will walk next to me and when I head to the bathroom, you join the group down there." Thank God, the plan worked!

I mingled with this group and looked around to figure out what to do next. An official in front was reviewing the tokens. I asked the man next to me, "What is he doing?" He just tears a corner off the token to verify it," he replied. I said, "Well I can do that!" and so I tore a corner off my token and sat pleased with myself. There I sat, after all, with all the men who had been admitted that morning!

We proceeded to the examination room. The American doctors checked us to make sure we were healthy and strong enough for farm work. They also inspected our hands to make sure that we had experience in the fields. I recognized a friend, named

Ramón, in line ahead of me. As the doctor examined his hands, I heard him ask, "What do you sell?" Ramón looked surprised and replied, "What do you mean?" I work in the field!" Luckily, they let him go through. After hearing that, I got down on my knees and rubbed my hands on the cement floor, just to make sure they looked rough enough. Lately, I had just been working as a musician. Worst of all, they also examined us for hemorrhoids. I felt sorry for the doctors, given that we had all been there for days without bathing.

I was relieved when I passed the physical exam. The last station was where they handed us our tickets for the trip north. We had to wait eight more days to board the train. Many men returned to their villages to say farewell to their families, but I stayed in Mexico City. I had already said my goodbyes to my family. Finally, the day came in April when we would all board the train for the United States. Nobody came to say goodbye to me, but I was aware that my friend Polonio had already told everyone that I was headed to the United States. On the train, we were all handed a paper bag with two sandwiches, an orange, and a soda. Three hours later we were given a second bag. I was very happy and comfortable, and I was excited to earn American dollars!

The train traveled through the American states and stopped at various cities. At each stop, the men who were needed to work in that town were instructed to get off. After three days on the train, I finally got off at the last stop, Idaho. I spotted the Americans, busy building the canvas tents that would be our camp for several months. The surroundings were beautiful, and I noticed a river nearby. José Romero, the contractor, told us that the river ran through the states of Idaho, Washington, and Oregon and that we could swim in it during our free time. He led us to a cafeteria where a large banquet awaited us. They served us eggs, milk, bread, oranges, and coffee. The contractor yelled out to get our attention. He explained the rules and warned us about our behavior because Braceros already had a bad reputation. He expected us to be on our best behavior. We were encouraged to eat as much as we wanted. Then he asked us if we wanted Mexican food and if any of us knew how to cook. Suddenly hands went up everywhere, but I doubted that they all knew how to cook. I recognized a man from Chapala, Jesús, who we nicknamed "El Chapeteado" because he had very red cheeks. I was surprised to see his hand up, but it was good to see a familiar face.

We were assigned our tents, and I slept soundly after the long train ride. The loud banging of pans very early in the morning woke us up for breakfast. We were well-fed, but I was not accustomed to eating three meals a day. Some braceros even gained weight during their time at camp.

I was up and ready for work on that first day. The contractor, José had told us to listen for our names and then to board the assigned truck. I don't know what happened because I never heard my name, and suddenly all the men were gone. José looked at me and asked, "What happened to you? I called all the names." I said, "I don't know, but I didn't hear my name." At that moment, a small truck arrived, and the driver announced that he needed two men, but since I was the only one, José sent me with him.

The cherry season was over, but the truck driver instructed me to glean the trees in an orchard. I picked whatever cherries were left after the previous pickers had finished working the orchard. The next day, the same man took me to a different orchard, and I spent the day there doing the same task. He didn't show up on the third day, so I was assigned to another group to pick peas. It was a difficult and slow task because the plants were so small. As we picked the peas, the trucks passed by, and we would throw the peas onto them. My partner and I couldn't take a break, so we put a big rock onto the conveyor belt and jammed it. Despite our best efforts, we only had a short break because the mechanics arrived and quickly repaired it. It was a long week!

Next, we were sent to the apple orchards where we were paid ten cents per box. Several men from our group were lucky because they were assigned the rows of trees that were full of big red apples. By the end of that first day, they filled 200 boxes. They were even able to do this without having to use ladders. Unfortunately, my co-worker and I got the orchard with mostly dry and small apples. I only filled between 40 to 50 boxes a day. One day, I filled 80 boxes, but nowhere near 200, the others filled. Several men were having accidents falling from the ladders. I was careful not to fall because I needed to stay healthy and keep earning dollars. I even began to consider the possibility of staying in the United States once my contract ended. Later, I approached José, the contractor, and asked him about it. Surprisingly, he said he could help me, and I felt hopeful.

Even though I had managed to not get hurt, I did get sick. I had been picking yellow apples and noticed that there were some large ones on the ground. During my break, I picked up a couple, rubbed them on my pants, and ate them, but when I returned to work my stomach began to ache and I vomited. José came running and asked me, "What happened? " I told him about the apples, and he said those were full of pesticides. He drove me back to the camp and a nurse gave me medicine and sent me back to my tent to rest. By the next day, I felt better, and José permitted me to return to work.

After the apple orchards, we worked at the plum orchards, which paid 20 cents per box. One morning, a truck arrived at the camp, full of more braceros. My friend said to me, "Hey, José, some strange, short men have arrived who aren't speaking Spanish." "Why do you say that, Santiago?" I asked. He responded, "Because I can't understand what they are saying! " I paid attention and realized that I, too, couldn't understand them. It turns out they were from the state of Oaxaca and spoke the Zapotec language. In the afternoon

I was working next to one of these men. At lunch he asked me how much he was going to get paid for each box, I told him 20 centavos. He continues, "I've picked ten boxes already, how much is that in pesos?" "Eight Mexican pesos," I answered. He yelled, "Well I no longer need to work! In Oaxaca, I only make eight pesos in one day!" Still, he continued working, and I realized that some of these men also spoke Spanish.

After the plum orchards, we moved to the potato fields, which meant more stoop labor for us. The machines had already dug up the potatoes which were strewn in the fields. Our job was to gather the potatoes and fill the sacks with two buckets of potatoes. One day we cheated and filled the sacks with only a bucket and a half. The next day, however, all of us were reprimanded. The owner rode up on his horse and yelled "Yesterday you filled many sacks, but we ended up with very few potatoes. I do not want this to happen again! " It didn't happen again.

Next, we were sent to another pea field, but this time we were paid 60 cents per basket. Again, it was difficult to fill the baskets. The workers were feeling frustrated and began to shout, "Strike! Strike!" "We struggled so much to get here," I thought, "and you are foolish enough to be saying these things!" That week we only worked three days and our checks were small, only 5, 6, or 8 dollars. Although we were charged a dollar a day for food and lodging, I was able to save some dollars.

A small town was within walking distance of our camp and there was no shortage of folks who were willing to give us a ride to or from the town. One Saturday, a large group of braceros went into town together. A handful of them got drunk and began fighting with each other. They made such a scene that the poor contractor was called to come and pick them up. I felt embarrassed for them because we had already been warned about how to behave. That night, the contractor had to make three trips to the bar to pick up the drunks. He warned them that if this happened again, they would be fired.

I had brought my violin to the States, and I practiced whenever I had time. It reminded me of playing with the mariachi, but I was still interested in staying in the States. I asked José Romero again about this and he said, "All you need is your birth certificate, and I'll help you." I smiled and imagined myself already as an American.

The next crop we worked on was sugar beet. It was back-breaking work, cutting the beet out of the ground with a sharp short hoe and slicing off the leaves. As the tractor passed, we threw the beets onto the conveyor belt. I was beginning to feel homesick, but kept thinking to myself, "Keep going, you are almost done." Many years later, I learned that in 1975, the short-handled hoe was outlawed due to efforts by Cesar Chavez and other organizations such as the CRLA (California Rural Legal Assistance).

November finally arrived, which meant we were close to the end of our contract. There were only two weeks left when an ominous snowstorm arrived. Due to the storm, we were moved from our canvas tent to a camp called Minikoda. It was one of the camps where the Japanese people had been interned. We stayed in the large cabins, and we were able to build fires inside to keep warm. It snowed the last two weeks when we worked in the sugar beet fields. I had never been so cold, and we did not have the proper attire for this weather. The falling snow would collect upon our backs and on our arms as we worked bent over. My hands would feel numb, and this experience made me change my mind about staying in the U.S. As soon as I had the opportunity, I spoke to José and told him, "It's very cold here. I am ready to return to Mexico" and that was the end of that. I completed my contract and was eager to leave like the rest of the men.

Camp Where the Japanese were Interned.

The braceros who had already completed their contract did not have to work the beets, but they had to wait for everyone to complete their contract before returning to Mexico. Finally, the day arrived when all of us had fulfilled them. That morning we were informed that the train would arrive at 11:00 am. The men were so excited that many of them did not even want to eat breakfast, but I did. The men began mocking the cooks, "We don't want your stinking chickens! We are going to Mexico, to eat real food! " What they called "stinking chickens" were the pheasants we were fed regularly, and we were all tired of them by this time.

The men were growing impatient and hungry because the train was late. I had saved two pieces of meat in my coat pockets just in case I got hungry later. The train arrived two hours late, but I did not go hungry.

I returned to Mexico City and met up with Mariachi Chapala. They were preparing to return to Chapala because María, Leopoldo's wife, was very ill. I could see that my brother was struggling financially and that they had barely enough to eat. I gave him fifty dollars and he was so grateful and excited. "Wow! I am going to the United States next year too!" he exclaimed.

For the time being, we were all back in Chapala. I ran into a man who had worked with me as a bracero in Idaho. He came to my house and said, "Look, José, I want to buy a house, but I don't have enough for it. I am short two hundred pesos. If you can lend me the money, I will pay you back with interest." The house cost eight hundred pesos, so I decided to help him. It took him a year to repay, but he faithfully paid me each month and paid with interest, as promised.

My brother Miguel married Petra, a childhood friend, at this time. They both came to live in the house with Leopoldo and his wife María. I headed to Mexico City again, leaving for two to three months each time and returning to Chapala to visit. Thankfully, I always found work.

Mariachi Chapala

I came back to work full-time with Mariachi Chapala, but between 1946 and 1948 we struggled to find work. We would go out to the plazas in the center of neighboring towns, but people simply did not have money. Once we were hired to serenade a woman for her birthday, but she did not respond to our music. When she finally opened her window, she threw a bucket of urine at us. My poor brother Miguel got most of it! Even worse, we never got paid and we were unable to locate the man who had hired us.

On another trip to Tijuana, we were all huddled together in a hotel room for a night. The owner passed by our room, and she saw how uncomfortable we were. The following day she spoke to us, "Boys come and eat with me and when you find work you can pay me." One of our guys had the idea to ask the Catholic priest if he would let us play after the evening Rosary, and he agreed. Regrettably, when we arrived with the large guitarrón and trumpets he exclaimed, "I thought you were going to play sacred music. Get out of here with all this noise!" So, we returned to our little hotel room. Another day with no work.

The mother of one of our violin players, Esteban Hernández, sold clothes in Chapala, and her business was becoming successful. She facilitated purchasing her items because she gave her clients credit so they could make payments periodically. Since we were stuck and did not know what to do, we asked Mrs. Hernández for a loan and promised to pay her once we returned to Chapala. She kindly sent us the money and we bought train tickets back to Chapala. The ride was long, and we had nothing to eat. A woman next to us from Tijuana told us that she was also headed to Guadalajara. Two men on board sold tequila by the glass and my friend and I combined our loose change to buy some. The woman from Tijuana looked at us timidly, so we offered her a drink. "Of course, I'd like a sip!" she said, eagerly. She told us that she had not eaten in three days, and I wished we had more to offer her.

Cananea, Sonora

In 1949 we ran into a man who was familiar with the U.S. border and the northern Mexican towns. He worked in the mining town of Cananea and informed us that there was lots of work there and that the people had money. "Let's go to Cananea if you want!" he exclaimed. "Well, why not!" We all agreed. Jesús Horta, our trumpeter, was married and concerned about leaving his wife and child, but he and the others decided to leave their wives in Guadalajara. They rented rooms for them in the same building so they could be together while we were out of town. We traveled to Cananea excited about the prospects of plentiful work.

On the way, we stopped in the town of Nayarit and visited the local radio station to see if they would allow us to play live on the air. They did, and we performed for two hours. As we were leaving the station, we saw a large crowd outside asking us to continue playing. Some folks had arrived on horseback and wanted us to leave with them. We explained that we could not stay because we were expected in Cananea. Our next stop was the town of Navojoa. The same thing happened there, we played at the local radio station and another crowd gathered outside.

We continued in this manner from town to town until we reached Cananea. Once there, we rented rooms in a large house so we could be together. We quickly established a good reputation and booked a lot of jobs! Cananea was not a big city. It was referred to as an American town because the mines at that time were American-owned; but the miners were Mexican and there were also many foreigners. It did not even look like a Mexican town, because the homes were A-frame and built from wood, like those in the States. Our mariachi was a success there, the public enjoyed our music, and they could afford to pay for it.

Agua Prieta, Sonora

We had been in Cananea for four weeks when a businessman from the border town of Agua Prieta arrived in a large fancy car. He said he had heard about us, and that he was looking for a mariachi for his business in Agua Prieta. "I have a restaurant bar and a large outdoor area. I can't afford to pay you; however, the people will pay to hear you. I have a hotel where you can stay at no cost." Shortly after his visit we left for Agua Prieta and checked into his hotel. The rooms were large and comfortable and there was enough room for two of us in each room.

We played every night and people came, including many young ladies. One afternoon Eva, my future wife, arrived with her mother. We noticed that the girls weren't drinking, they just came to hear us because we were a novelty. The previous mariachi did not know many songs, but our mariachi was able to play everything the audience requested. The outdoor patio was huge, and everyone danced, but I noticed that Eva didn't.

We were in Agua Prieta from April until September of 1949, playing every night. A member of our group, Lupe Zavala, met and married a girl from there, María. We threw a party for the wedding couple with sodas and beers and played for them and their guests. Once again, everyone was dancing except Eva. My brother Leopoldo said, "Why don't you dance with that young girl? She's the only one not dancing." Well, I danced with her and joked with her about stepping on my toes. From dancing and talking, we got to know each other. During the day, sometimes we would go to the movies, along with her mother, of course. Eva's eldest brother, Manuel, came to meet me because he had heard that I had been visiting with his little sister. We turned out to be good friends. In later years, I used to tease my wife and tell her that things had gone sour for me in Agua Prieta because I had met her there and ended up married. She always ignored my jokes.

September was ending and it was time for us to leave Agua Prieta. Lupe Zavala took his new wife and his mother-in-law back to Cananea in a separate car from ours. I said farewell to Eva, who said that she wanted to come with me. I promised her that I would come back for her. I think she didn't believe me because a couple of weeks later, Lupe yelled at me and said, "José, here comes your family," and then he laughed. I came out of my room and was shocked to see Eva and her mother, Doña Rita. They had traveled to Cananea and I learned how risky their trip had been because they had not traveled much before.

Doña Rita's purse had been stolen, and they had not eaten for hours. Doña Rita made a big sacrifice leaving everything behind to come with Eva, her youngest child.

Eva and I made plans to marry in Cananea, but we had to wait. The judge in Cananea reprimanded me for wanting to marry such a young girl, because Eva was only 14 years old. My friends suggested that we go to Nogales, and that is where we were finally wed. Afterward, our group traveled to the town of Magdalena. We wanted to get there in time for the festivities. The fiesta lasted three days, and we were busy working the entire time.

Next stop, Guadalajara!

My compadre Chuy (Jesús Horta) had received a letter from his wife Conchita. She had been concerned about his extended absence and was now waiting for him in Nogales with her daughter. The other spouses were also worried since they had remained alone in Guadalajara for such a long time. I hoped that Eva and her mother would adjust to living there, and to being married to a musician. This was one of the reasons that I had put off getting married. Things were different in the north compared to central Mexico. One simple difference was the tortillas, which in the north were made from white flour versus the corn tortillas of Guadalajara. Also, most of the women wore rebozos, something Eva had never done.

In Guadalajara, since our rooms were all next to each other, Eva and her mother met the other wives. One afternoon, Eva was alone when a young woman named Emilia arrived. She was the daughter of Doña Leandra, whom we knew from Chapala. Leopoldo had gone to Chapala, and he had mentioned to me that Emilia was coming to see him in Guadalajara and that they planned to marry. María, Leopoldo's first wife, had died and his in-laws were taking care of his daughter Angelita. We were not working in Guadalajara very long before the opportunity to play in Mexicali, Baja California presented itself.

Mexicali, Another Border Town

In 1950 we ran into a man in Guadalajara, whom I had met before, named Mr. Amezcua. He also happened to be the father of José Amezcua, a guitar player I met many years later in Stockton, California. Mr. Amezcua informed us that he had been to Mexicali. There he had met the owner of a restaurant/bar who had expressed interest in obtaining a mariachi from Guadalajara for his business. My brother Leopoldo had taken over managing the mariachi, so he sent a letter to the bar owner expressing our interest. Once he negotiated a deal, he sent us 2000 pesos to travel by train to Mexicali with our families. The trip took two days.

Eva and I did not have any children, but my mother-in-law, Doña Rita, traveled with us. Eva and I were already legally married, but it was in Mexicali where we finally got married in the church, alongside Leopoldo and Emilia. Doña Rita was a talented seamstress, and she made the two brides green wedding dresses, which they wore to the Cathedral. The women walked up front, eager to get to the Cathedral, with Leopoldo and I following behind.

While in Guadalajara, we met a young violinist named Nati Cano. He was from a small rural town near Guadalajara, Ahuisculco. We were impressed with him and invited him to join our mariachi and come with us to Mexicali. His family was distraught at the thought of Nati moving so far, Later, however, his family joined him up north.

Another violinist and excellent singer, Heriberto Molina, also joined our group. He played with us for a couple of years and then returned to play with Mariachi Vargas, the most well-known mariachi in Mexico. Heriberto made hundreds of recordings throughout his career. Recordings he made with us were later re-released on an album, Los Dos Palomos (The Two Doves) in which he sang with Ricardo González. There are at least three other LPs where Heriberto sang with Mariachi Chapala.

Album cover for Los Dos Palomos

Mariachi Chapala accompanying Lola Beltrán.

José playing the harp with Mariachi Chapala.

In Mexicali, the mariachi already had four violinists, so I switched to playing the harp. Leopoldo played the guitarrón, the large acoustic bass guitar, and Miguel continued playing the guitar. We didn't have a car, so Leopoldo asked the owner of the cantina, called Bar Monterrey, to help us obtain a station wagon or a van. He went across the border to Calexico and purchased a used station wagon for $400 dollars. It was large enough for all of us and our instruments, and we repaid him after we had saved enough cash.

Tarzan was the owner of the Bar Monterey in Mexicali. He also helped us find lodging and Eva and I rented a small room where we lived for a brief time with Doña Rita. We had few furnishings, and when we needed a table, we flipped over our big, round metal bathtub. A few months later, Leonardo, Eva's brother, and his two friends came to visit Doña Rita, but our room was so small that Doña Rita and I had to join them outside. I felt bad about this situation. Also, the location was not secure, which was important since I was gone most nights working, so this motivated me to find another place.

We performed at the Bar Monterey every night and charged a peso and fifty centavos per song. The crowd consisted of regulars made up of cotton pickers and other laborers who crossed the border for work. If there were agricultural jobs, we would have had an audience willing to pay for our music. I learned that the harvested cotton crop does not spoil, and that, unlike fresh produce, it can be stored until its value rises. Mexicali is in Mexico's northern desert area, and in the 1950's, to irrigate the crops the farmers brought water in from the Colorado River. Due to droughts, however, ranchers were forced to sell their land and farmers also faced plagues from insects and other pests.

Eva and I eventually moved to a more spacious and safer room, but still without running water. Every week, the water truck filled the huge cement tubs located outside our rooms.

We paid for the water we needed for drinking, bathing, and washing our clothes. It was in this new space that our first daughter, Carmen, was born in 1951. However, she was stillborn, and we buried her in the local Mexicali Cemetery. This was a sad time for us, especially for Eva who was alone. Doña Rita was away visiting her family in Agua Prieta and had not returned in time for the birth.

When Doña Rita returned with her husband Don Antonio, I rented them their own room. We realized that Don Antonio was very ill. He had stayed back in Agua Prieta with his sons and worked on the ranch of his eldest son Manuel. Manuel was very intelligent and an excellent mechanic who made a good living with his auto business. Being the eldest, Manuel helped his brothers with their businesses, and he always looked out for his parents. He had acquired a ranch by trading his brand-new car for the ranch. The young ranch owner had prioritized the new car over his ranch. Manuel and I were close, and he also played the violin, so I gifted him a beautiful antique violin. He had invited me to his ranch, and I was eager to visit. To get there, we had to cross a wide river which would sometimes flood during the rainy season. Unfortunately, when we arrived the river was overflowing and we couldn't cross it, so I never got to see his ranch.

Don Antonio died in October of 1951 in Mexicali. Everyday Doña Rita would stop by the house of a neighbor, Carolina, on her way to run errands. One day after the family had buried Don Antonio, Carolina gave her condolences to Doña Rita. She mentioned that her real father was also named Antonio and that he was from the state of Sonora. After a long discussion, they realized that Carolina was indeed Don Antonio's daughter from his first marriage. What a pity that she never met him while he was alive. From then on, everyone was very happy to include Carolina as part of Doña Rita's close-knit family.

In 1952, I met a man named Don Pancho who came around to inform us that he was going to build new rooms of cement blocks with wood doors and glass windows. I requested that he reserve a room for my family, as did Jesús Horta and Esteban Hernández from the mariachi. We moved in as soon as they were completed and then our daughter, Olivia, was born. Carolina gifted us with two chickens to cook and make a broth for Eva to help her recuperate after giving birth. Doña Rita always had visitors because she had eight children and lots of grandchildren. She had 14 children, but only eight had survived. Three months after Olivia was born, Doña Rita took Eva and Olivia to Agua Prieta to visit her family. Upon returning a month later they brought along Juan, Eva's youngest brother, and Ernestina, Eva's cousin who was the same age as Eva. Juan stayed in Mexicali and soon met and married Esperanza. Ernestina stayed just a couple of months, then returned to Agua Prieta. Eva's older sister Rita also came to live in Mexicali with her husband Ramón and their children. Doña Rita, being a widow, decided to remain permanently in Mexicali with her daughters Eva and Rita.

Meanwhile, I had been saving money to buy a plot of land for a house in Mexicali. I eventually saved enough to buy one in the new Baja California neighborhood. The designated land had been valued at 150,000 pesos. I gathered the needed buyers, and a doctor assisted with the legal documents. Each one of the buyers paid 300 pesos per lot, but the corner parcels were more expensive. The new landowners, including myself, helped to measure the streets and place the surveyor poles on each lot. Mine turned out to be next to a canal, which I did not want. When I went to the office to request a different lot, I was told that I could not change it. So, I decided to purchase two more lots, the one next to mine and the one behind it, for more privacy. I lent Leopold money so that he could also buy a parcel in that vicinity. When I received my deed, I began construction and hired a couple of men to help me. I was eager to move in as soon as the walls went up, but the roof was still missing, so I had to be patient.

My mariachi companions didn't want to purchase lots in the Baja California area because they did not trust the salespeople. Fortunately, we did not have any problems. Four of the mariachi members—Esteban, Agustín, Jesús, and Miguel—bought land in another neighborhood, Colonia Nueva Esperanza. Their lots were all on the same block, so it was easier for them to stay in contact. These lots were more expensive, at a thousand pesos each, because they had water. My brother Miguel's house was built by our nephew, Benjamin Aguila Sosa (son of my sister Micaela).

In 1954, our first son, José (Joe), was born. That same year, Doña Leandra and Cristina, Leopoldo's mother-in-law, and sister-in-law, arrived from Chapala because Doña Leandra's husband had died. They stayed in Mexicali with Leopoldo and Emilia, but Cristina moved out when she married shortly after.

When my nephew, Benjamin, arrived in Mexicali he was only 14 years old. He had traveled on foot from the mountains down to the ranchito of Loma Alta, and finally to Chapala. After that trek, he traveled to Guadalajara and then by train to Mexicali. He told us that his mother, my sister Micaela, had died and that his grandfather had taken the responsibility of caring for his younger siblings. Magdalena, Benjamin's sister, telephoned us to find out if Benjamin had arrived safely. Micaela had lived in the mountains far from Loma Alta where we had grown up. When she was young, she had been kidnapped and forced to marry the man who stole her. This happened sometimes back in those days.

Benjamin stayed with Leopoldo and Emilia until Doña Leandra arrived. He became a mason and was good at construction until he retired in Mexicali. He never married, but my brother Miguel (his godfather) visited him often after Leopoldo and I left for Los Angeles.

**The four Sosa brothers: Ramón, José, Miguel, and
Leopoldo**

Shopping with Eva in Mexicali.

Music in Mexicali

Tarzan, the owner of the, Bar Monterrey, was a good businessman. He had us play every night for five years and kept us informed of parties and events taking place elsewhere so we could supplement our earnings. The bartender there even became my brother Leopoldo's compadre. We were grateful for all the opportunities we had been provided: leaving Guadalajara, obtaining transportation, finding housing, and eventually becoming homeowners, all thanks to Tarzan's help.

When we played at weddings and parties for the wealthy, we were never contracted for a specific number of hours. Sometimes we played all through the night. For a while, we even worked for the first governor of Baja California, Braulio Maldonado Sández. All the Mexicali police officers knew where we lived, and they would come around and pick us up whenever the governor requested our mariachi. One time the officers took us all the way to Ensenada without informing us, and none of us had brought enough money for the weekend. Even though we charged him the minimum, the governor had not paid us for quite some time. By now, he owed us more than a thousand pesos. One of his employees informed the secretary that Mr. Sández needed to pay us, and he directed her to give us a check for two thousand 2000 pesos. Needless to say, we were relieved and delighted. The following day Emilia, Leopoldo's wife, went to cash the check at the government palace. They explained to her that no one in the office could cash it. They asked her to sign the check and told her to return the next day. Unfortunately, when Emilia returned, she was informed that they did not have the check and that they did not know what she was talking about. It was disappointing and frustrating to know that the government officials had been dishonest and corrupt. There was nothing we could do—it was their word against ours. We had always gotten paid in cash, so we were unfamiliar with the process of cashing a check.

After this incident, the police officers stopped coming around for us. But overall, we did well in Mexicali because we were able to get ahead and establish a reputation as a good mariachi.

We performed regularly on the Mexicali radio station XEAA. The station would usually draw a crowd of people who came to hear the performers. Mexicali Beer sponsored the program, so they aired their commercials every day at 11:30 in the morning, right before we played. This opportunity provided us with the privilege of accompanying many of the popular musical artists of the time, including José Alfredo Jimenez, Miguel Aceves Mejía, Lola Beltrán, Gilberto Valenzuela, and others. There were other mariachis in town, but they did not have the fancy mariachi outfits we had, which were professionally made for us in Tijuana.

Mariachi Chapala at the radio station in Mexicali. (Previoius page): Left to right: José Sosa, Agustín Cervantes, Nati Cano, Esteban Hernández, Heriberto Molina, Leopoldo Sosa, Miguel Sosa, Ricardo González, Lupe Ledesma, and Jesús Horta

Left to Right: José Sosa, Agustín Cervantes, Nati Cano, Esteban Hernández, Heriberto Molina, Leopoldo Sosa, Miguel Sosa, Ricardo González, Lupe Ledesma, and Jesús Horta.

Mariachi Chapala accompanying José Alfredo Jiménez.

Top row: Nati Cano, José Sosa, Jesús Horta, Miguel Sosa and Agustín Cervantes.
Bottom row: Trinidad Diestras, Lupe Ledesma, Ricardo González, Leopoldo Sosa, and Esteban Hernández.

**Mariachi Chapala accompanying Fernando Valenzuela.
Left to Right: Heriberto Molina, Esteban Hernández,
Nati Cano, José Sosa, Jesús Horta, Miguel Sosa, Ricardo
González, Lupe Ledesma, and Leopoldo Sosa**

Los Angeles

The singer Miguel Aceves Mejía was immensely popular in the 1950s and was given a contract to perform at the Million Dollar Theater in Los Angeles. His only stipulation on the contract was to ensure that Mariachi Chapala accompanied him, so off we went to Los Angeles. It was 1955.

We learned that the Million Dollar Theater was founded in 1918 and was one of the first theaters to feature Mexican and Latin American variety shows in the United States. Between the 1940's and the 1960's, popular artists of the times performed there, such as Pedro Infante, Jorge Negrete, Dolores Del Río, Cantinflas, Agustín Lara, María Félix, and José Alfredo Jiménez.

While in Los Angeles, Miguel Aceves Mejía was invited to perform at the Club Granada, an acclaimed restaurant and bar on Broadway Avenue in downtown Los Angeles. The owner, José Chavez, really appreciated our music and offered us a six-month contract, to which Leopoldo agreed. First, we had to wait to get our work permits to work legally in the United States. With our permits, Mr. Chávez wrote up a contract for payments of $50 a week per musician, including hotel rooms and a daily meal at his restaurant.

Poster for the mariachi at the Granada

Million Dollar Theatre in the 1970s, featuring Pedro Rey, son of Esteban Hernández (original member of Mariachi Chapala)

To acquire the work permits, we traveled to Agua Prieta, and then to Nogales, where we remained for a week working with a contractor named Rubén. He was a friend of Mr. Chávez, and he arranged our documents for Los Angeles. Mr. Chávez paid all the expenses for us up front, and we repaid him later. After we completed our commitment to the singer Miguel Aceves Mejía, the ten of us returned to Los Angeles, this time with our work permits. The six months passed quickly, and on our last day at the restaurant, the place was packed with loyal customers. Everyone thought we would be leaving because we had expressed our eagerness to return to Mexicali and our families. Mr. Chávez asked us to remain for another six months, but we requested a leave to visit our families first. After our visit to Mexicali, we went to Tijuana to obtain another permit. Incidentally, Mr. Chávez knew the head of the immigration office, so we were easily granted the necessary permits. His restaurant was doing very well, and the customers liked our music, so he increased our salary by $10. We renewed our contracts for another two years, and each time we renewed our contracts, he raised our salaries.

One day, before heading to work at Club Granada, I went to a corner store to pick up some items. I saw a poster announcing a mariachi called Mariachi Reyes de Chapala. I scrutinized the poster and realized that I did not recognize any of the musicians as being from Chapala! The poster announced that this mariachi would be performing at one of the Spanish-language television stations (which frequently rented a few hours from the English Language stations). Years later, a friend who had spoken to one of the members of this mariachi confirmed that it was true, none of the members were from Chapala. The name was given to them by a man who was sponsoring the group, and they just kept the name, even though none of them were from that area! Mariachi Reyes de Chapala was probably the first group to broadcast on American radio.

On March 7, 1957, we were granted permanent U.S. resident status and received our green cards. We continued to perform at Club Granada until 1960. Mr. Chávez's assistance in arranging these documents, for each of us and our families, was greatly appreciated. He wrote a letter in which he committed to sponsoring and taking financial responsibility for us. Mr. Chávez paid $500 for each of our documents, and after six months, we were able to pay him back. The only one who did not want permanent U.S. residency was my brother, Miguel, despite our efforts to try to convince him to come with us. Miguel returned to his family in Mexicali and continued to play with other mariachis in that town.

In December 1959, my family crossed the border. I had purchased an old car and borrowed a trailer to haul some of our furniture. I took Eva and our children: Olivia 7, José 5, Lalo 3, and Manuel was only 1 year old. My brother-in-law Ramón, who lived in San Pedro, California, arranged the residency documents for my mother-in-law, Doña Rita.

Our elderly friend, María, and her husband had lived on my property in Mexicali. I had helped build their adobe house when I first met them. The couple didn't pay rent because they didn't have any family to help them. While living there, they had become very attached to my son Eduardo (Lalo). They were distraught when they found out that we were moving to Los Angeles. They asked if they could buy Lalo from us. I assured them that we couldn't do such a thing and they cried terribly when we finally left. Eva's sister, Rita, and her family moved into our home, and we sold it when they immigrated to the United States a few years later. Mr. Chávez had been covering the cost of our hotel rooms, but when our families arrived, we had to seek our own lodging. Leopoldo and his family had arrived a few months before we did, and he was already renting a home in Los Angeles. My family stayed with him for a couple of months, until I got an apartment near downtown Los Angeles. It was at this time that we were informed that our son José (Joe) had been diagnosed with tuberculosis. We were grateful that none of our other children were infected. José was removed from our family and placed in the Olive View Sanatorium, in the San Fernando area. Eva and I visited him at the hospital as often as we could, usually every 1–2 weeks. When José was first hospitalized, he didn't speak English. But a year later, when he was cured and released, he couldn't speak Spanish! Olivia, however, was already in school and learning English, so she translated as much as she could until José began to speak some Spanish again.

When we were looking for a place to live, a friend of Mr. Chávez told us, "Look, there are some government projects in East Los Angeles and the rent is affordable, depending on your income." A group of us followed up on this lead, and Leopold, Agustín, Esteban, Jesús Horta, and I were granted apartments in the Maravilla Projects in East Los Angeles. All our families lived close to each other there. My youngest son Victor was born in the Los Angeles County General Hospital, so he was automatically a U.S. citizen. He was also the only one of my children born in a hospital: my other four children had all been born at home. We eventually had to leave the projects and find another place to rent. I remained in Los Angeles because it was easier to live in a Latino community, where all the services we needed were available in Spanish. By that time, Los Angeles had a Spanish-language television channel, KMEX channel 34, and several Spanish-language radio stations.

In 1960 we recorded an album titled *Mariachi Americana*, for which we were paid $500 dollars each. It was a bilingual album with some songs in English and some in Spanish. We were photographed at the Santa Monica Pier in our Charros outfits for the album cover. The professional singers were Rita "La Bonita" and her husband, Antonio DeMarco. The couple was very popular and were the number one team on the Spanish-speaking language radio station, KWKW, in Los Angeles. Another featured singer on the album was Fernando Paniagua, photographed in the Center of the album photo with no instrument.

Esteban Hernández, Agustín Cervantes, Nati Cano, Jesús Horta, José Sosa, unnamed trumpet player, Trinidad Diestras, José Amezcua, Ricardo González, and Leopoldo Sosa.

Front of the álbum.

Back of our "Mariachi Americana" album.

I never knew why it was called Mariachi Americana instead of Mariachi Americano. The back cover explains that this album was "another big step towards international understanding through music." *Americana* is defined as: "A genre of American music having roots in early folk and country music." **(3. Merriam-Webster Dictionary)** All I can assume is that it was a reference to the fact that California once was part of Mexico and that some of that culture and music was still relevant.

After the album, we were invited to play in a movie starring Elvis Presley, *Fun in Acapulco*. We were driven to the movie studio, and they asked to borrow our mariachi outfits. Members from Mariachi Los Vaqueros and Mariachi Águila were already there. They were included in the film, but our group was not. We did, however, get to see Elvis acting and lip-syncing his songs near a swimming pool. About two weeks later they returned our suits, nicely pressed, and cleaned. I did not watch the movie until years later when it was on TV.

Advertisement for Fun in Acapulco

Leopoldo Sosa, director of Mariachi Chapala and later of Mariachi Los Jilgueros.

End of an Era

Leopoldo received a message from a man in Seattle, Washington who was looking for a well-known mariachi from Los Angeles. He had heard about Mariachi Chapala and invited us to play at the 1962 World's Fair, to be held in Seattle. Leopoldo decided to go, but most of the members did not agree with this decision. Seattle was far away, and some of the original members of our mariachi had already left the group. In the end, Mariachi Chapala broke apart. I and the other bandmates joined other local mariachis.

Leopoldo and Jesús were the only two who left for Seattle with their families, hoping to recruit other musicians once they arrived in Seattle. Instead, they had a difficult time because the man who hired them did not comply with the contract and did not pay them accordingly. It was also difficult to find other musicians who could play mariachi music in that part of the country. After the World's Fair, Leopoldo and Jesus returned to California and settled in San Francisco.

About ten months later, I traveled to San Francisco with another mariachi and ran into Leopoldo and Jesus playing in a bar. They told me that they were planning to leave San Francisco soon and move to Stockton, a town better suited for their young families. Once in Stockton, Leopoldo formed a new mariachi, Los Jilgueros, which included Leopoldo, guitarron player, Jesús Horta and Lupe Horta, both trumpet players, Jose Diaz, vocalist and guitarist, and David Rodriguez, vocalist and vihuela player. Both Jose Diaz and David still play with the Jilgueros. Many other members have come and gone, and many are now deceased. I continued to work in Los Angeles with other mariachis but in 1965 I moved my family to Santa Ana. I had obtained a job at the Randolph Rubber Company, which made tennis shoes, in the city of Garden Grove. I found other mariachis in the Santa Ana area and played with them on the weekends, at parties, weddings, funerals, and quinceañeras. Unfortunately, this left me little time with my five children who were growing up quickly, but my wife and mother-in-law were always there. Later I was able to get my wife a job at the same factory and fortunately, my mother-in-law remained at home with the children.

When Nati Cano left Mariachi Chapala he joined Mariachi Águila, which later became Los Camperos. Miguel Martinez, considered the greatest mariachi trumpet player, had played with the famous Mariachi Vargas since 1942, and briefly played with Mariachi Águila in the 1960s. Six months later, Nati took the leadership for Los Camperos because the previous leader, José Frías, had died in an automobile accident in Mexico. The very first album by Los Camperos, in 1960 does not yet include Nati's name in the credits. Los Camperos became a very well-known mariachi and Nati opened a popular restaurant, La Fonda, in Los Angeles. Frank Fouce Jr., who had managed the Million Dollar Theatre, became his partner, and helped him select the best site for the restaurant. Mr. Fouce also created the architectural design for La Fonda restaurant. Buses, full of tourists, regularly traveled to La Fonda to hear authentic mariachi music until it closed.

In the early 1990s, under the leadership of Nati Cano, Los Camperos recorded an album with Linda Ronstadt, *Canciones de Mi Padre,* (Songs of my Father), and a second album with her was titled *Más Canciones* (More Songs). Los Camperos toured with her afterwards and have since toured the world due to their popularity. Linda was a well-known pop singer, and after these successful Spanish albums, she was recognized as a popular Latina singer.

In 2012, the last time Nati's group played in Stockton, California, my daughter took me to the concert. I went backstage with my friend Jonathan Clark (a mariachi historian) and had a chance to speak to Nati. He told me that he was retiring soon due to health reasons, and he introduced me to Jesús (Chuy) Guzmán, the man who would be taking his place. Jonathan took a photo of the three of us. When the concert began, Nati came to the microphone, welcomed everyone, and introduced me. He asked me to stand up to be recognized and stated that he was forever grateful to me and my brother Leopoldo for asking him to join Mariachi Chapala back in 1950, and for bringing him to Mexicali and then to Los Angeles, where he had the great opportunity to work with us and later Los Camperos. It was very touching, and I wish my brother Leopoldo had been alive to listen to Nati's comments.

Esteban Hernández, who had been with the mariachi since its early days in Chapala, had sons who continued the mariachi tradition and formed their own groups. His eldest son, better known as Pedro Rey, became a very successful singer, instrumentalist, and band leader. Both Chencho (Crescencio) and his brother Pedro played with Los Camperos at different times.

José backstage with his old partner, Nati Cano, in 2011 in Stockton, CA. In the middle, the new leader for Mariachi Los Camperos, Jesús Guzmán.

Later, both also played with Mariachi Vargas! As members of this mariachi, the brother became one of the earliest trumpet duos in that group. Two other brothers, Antonio a trumpet player, and Humberto (Beto) a guitar player, also mariachi musicians, played with Mariachi Los Galleros.

Pedro Rey and Los Galleros made many recordings and also had a restaurant, El Rey in Montebello. This restaurant, and La Fonda restaurant, were unique in that they were the only two restaurants that presented live mariachi music and where the mariachis themselves owned the restaurants and were the primary attraction. This was true for a few years in the early 1970s, When Pedro Rey returned to Chapala, and word got out that he was there, many mariachi musicians came and asked him to sing with them, but more than anything else they asked him to rehearse their groups.

José Hernández is the youngest son of Esteban. He formed the world-renowned Mariachi Sol de México, and his brother Antonio joined the group. His brother Chuy was also a member of this mariachi from its inception. This mariachi is recognized all over the world and they have made many recordings. José Hernandez also had a very popular restaurant, *Cielito Lindo*, in South El Monte. When Esteban died in 1997, Leopold and I attended his funeral in Los Angeles. All his sons and many other mariachi musicians accompanied Esteban to his funeral. At the cemetery, Leopoldo stood next to the coffin and sang, dedicating the song, "God Never Dies", *(Dios Nunca Muere)* to his compadre Esteban. It was a very special tribute.

When our brother Miguel died in Mexicali in 1972, Leopoldo called me in Santa Ana and said, "Come to Stockton, we're the last two left of our family." Eva agreed and we rented our house to a relative in Santa Ana and moved to Stockton. We brought Manuel, Lalo (Eduardo), and Victor. Joe had already moved out and was living in San Diego. Olivia was already in Stockton, staying with Leopold and Emilia while attending college. It happened again that a couple who lived across the street from us in Santa Ana asked us to leave Eduardo with them. They were very fond of him; however, it was not an option, we also wanted him with us. We stayed in Leopoldo's home for a couple of months until we found an affordable house to purchase, thereby committing to stay in Stockton, so we sold our house in Santa Ana.

The first house we bought in Stockton was in the old section of town, on Sutter Street. It was built in 1906 and it was the only one-story house, surrounded by huge 2-story homes. I would practice my violin in the backyard, surrounded by huge trees full of birds. When I decided to sell the Sutter St. house and placed a For Sale sign out front, one of our neighbors came to visit. She said she was sad to see us leave because we were good neighbors, and mostly because she had enjoyed listening to me practice the violin.

In Stockton, I played the violin with the mariachi Los Jilgueros from 1972 to 2008. For years, Los Jilgueros was popular and well-known in Stockton and throughout Northern California. In addition to working as a musician, a friend of Leopoldo, Mr. Solís, had a cleaning service and hired me as a custodian at the Sharpe Army Depot in nearby Lathrop, California. I retired from that job when I turned 65 in 1983, but as always, I continued with Los Jilgueros, even after my brother Leopoldo passed away in 2003. The Jilgueros still exist today, but there are also many other mariachi groups in the San Joaquin County area now. The mariachi tradition continues!

In 2006, Eva and I moved to Elk Grove where our daughter Olivia lived. We bought a house near hers and sold another one of our houses in Stockton. We have been very comfortable here because our neighborhood was very quiet and peaceful. Two of my sons, Manuel and Eduardo, live within an hour's drive. However, we rarely get to see our other two sons often because Joe retired in Vietnam and Victor lives in Texas with his family. I am grateful for my family and pleased that they are all doing well.

I am appreciative that Eva decided to follow me to the United States and always supported me and our family. I am thankful to God for having given me so many years of life and, although I went through difficult times, I cannot complain. I have had a good life, a good wife and family, and the gift of music—which I loved from an early age. Thanks be to God!

The End

"Los Güeros", brothers Leopoldo, Miguel and José Sosa

Mariachi Los Jilgueros in the 1990's: José Diaz, David Rodriguez, Leopoldo Sosa, Armando Rodriguez, José Sosa, Beto and Miguel Rios. Jose Diaz was inducted into Stockton's Mexican American Hall of Fame (2016).

Los Jilgueros playing with Tony Orlando on his Spanish song tour in Lake Tahoe. Left to Right: José Sosa, Tony, Armando Rodríguez and David Rodríguez

Los Jilgueros with Oscar De La Hoya
Left to Right: José Barron, Freddy Gallardo, Leopoldo Sosa, Armando Rodriguez, José Sosa, David Rodriguez and José Diaz. Jose Barron was inducted into Stockton's Mexican-American Hall of Fame (2005).

Los Jilgueros: Veronica, Francisco, José Diaz, David Rodriguez, Artemio Anguiano, José Barron, and Aurelio Salcedo.The last time José played with his Mariachi colleagues because he died later that month in August 2013.

José and Eva celebrating their October birthdays.
They were married for almost 64 years.

He enjoyed walking and when he could no longer walk, he
rode his bike.
Loving nature and being outdoors.

SAN JOAQUIN DELTA COLLEGE
DELTAS LOS MESTENOS
MARIACHI CONCERT
HONORS JOSE SOSA
SAT MAY 15 7 30 PM
ATHERTON AUDITORIUM CALL 954-5110

José and Leopoldo Sosa were inducted into Stockton's Mexican American Hall of Fame in 2010 for their contributions to music and culture and for their service to the community.

MARIACHI CHAPALA MEMBERS: R.I.P.
Miguel Sosa 1972
Esteban Hernández 1997
Leopoldo Sosa 2003
Jesús Horta 2010
José Sosa 2013
Nati Cano 2014
Agustín Cervantes 2018
Heriberto Molina 2022

GLOSSARY

ranchito – *a small group of homes in the countryside*
güero/güera – *a person of light skin and features*
centavo – *Mexican cent (100 centavos = 1 peso)*
petate – *woven straw mats used for sleeping on the ground*
comál –*a smooth flat griddle*
capulín tree – *like a cherry tree*
agave – *a succulent species with fleshy leaves (local name maguey, used to make mezcal liquor)*
peso – *Mexican currency*
pulque – *Mexican alcoholic drink made by fermenting nectar from the maguey plant*
sombrero – *wide brimmed hat*
rebozo - *shawl*
kilo – *1 kilo = 2.2 pounds*
pozole – *means hominy, it is a soup made with hominy and meat*
compadre/comadre – *what you call your child's godparents*
guitarrón – *a large, acoustic bass guitar*

ACKNOWLEDGMENT

83

I am forever grateful to Mr. Jonathan Clark, mariachi musician and historian. He became a friend of my father, and they shared their love of mariachi music and its history. Jonathan helped to edit this book and he encouraged me to finish it. My friend Richard Soto, also helped with the proof reading and facilitated his Chicano Research Center for the presentation of the Spanish edition of this book. My cousin Jesus was helpful in clarifying some of the information included in this book. ¡GRACIAS!

ABOUT THE AUTHOR

Olivia Sosa earned a master's degree in Multilingual/ Multicultural Education from the University of the Pacific in Stockton, California. She was a bilingual teacher for 16 years and then moved on to Teacher Education and Administration. She was Director of Migrant Education and then Director of the Multilingual/ Multicultural Education Program in the San Joaquin County Office of Education, also serving on several education committees for the California Department of Education. She retired in 2013 after 38 years in the field of education. Olivia was born in Mexicali, Baja California, Mexico and immigrated to the US, with her family, when she was 7 years old. Her volunteer work includes translating the curriculum for the Spanish-speaking grief support groups, and facilitating these groups since 2017, as well as participating in political activism activities in her community.

www.ingramcontent.com/pod-product-compliance
Lightning Source LLC
Chambersburg PA
CBHW020628160726
47991CB00002B/951